MY KARMIC DHARMA
A Journey Through My Autistic Son

Dr. Pankajam Rangarajan, MD (Radiologist)

Acknowledgment

My heartfelt gratitude begins with my mother, whose quiet strength, unconditional love, and spiritual presence have been the unwavering force in my life. Her resilience has been my refuge during the most trying moments of this journey.

To Anusha, my precious niece -your boundless love for Ashwin, your innate ability to connect with him, and your joyful spirit have been a gift to both him and me. You bring light wherever you go.

To my sisters and brothers, each of whom has offered their unique form of support ,whether through presence, advice, or silent understanding — thank you for walking beside me with compassion and strength.

To my husband, who has stood through the highs and lows of parenting with me, thank you for your shared endurance and commitment.

To my entire family, whose collective love has held me through the tides of uncertainty — this book carries all your fingerprints.

Your support ,spoken, felt, and sometimes just quietly known has helped me rise again and again. This journey is mine, but I never walked it alone.

Copyright

Copyright © 2025 by Dr. Pankajam Rangarajan

All rights reserved. No part of this book may be reproduced or transmitted in any form or by any means, electronic or mechanical, including photocopying, recording, or by any information storage and retrieval system, without written permission from the author.

Self-published by the author in India.

Dedication

To Ashwin — the light of my life and the mirror of my soul.
And to every parent walking the invisible road with courage.

Some souls arrive in our lives not to be healed but to heal us — not through cures, but through a deep transformation of the heart. Ashwin's arrival was not an accident, nor a genetic error — it was a karmic invitation to discover grace in the midst of difficulty, and divinity in the day-to-day reality of autism. This book is not a medical journal. It is a soul journal. And it is offered with folded hands.

I am not a writer by profession. I am a Radiologist. A mother. A seeker. And this book was born not from ambition but from necessity — the necessity to share what I've seen, felt, learned, and survived while walking this path with my son, Ashwin. May this book find its way to every parent who needs to feel less alone, and every heart that seeks a deeper meaning in what appears unfair.

Table of Contents

Foreword .... pg 6

Preface .... pg 7

Chapter 1: Birth & NICU Days .... pg 8

Chapter 2: Hearing Loss & Autism Diagnosis .... pg 10

Chapter 3: Building Inner Strength .... pg 12

Chapter 4: Societal Stigma and Support .... pg 14

Chapter 5: Medical Struggles and Breakthroughs .... pg 16

Chapter 6: Graceful Turns & Divine Help .... pg 18

Chapter 7: Autism and Hypersexuality .... pg 20

Chapter 8: The Pillars Who Stood Tall .... pg 22

Chapter 9: Vedic Insight – Why Ashwin Was Born This Way .... pg 24

Chapter 10: Radiologist's Perspective on Autism .... pg 26

Chapter 11: Final Words to Fellow Parents .... pg 28

About the Author .... pg 30

Tailpiece .... pg 31

Picture pathway… … … … … … pg 32

Chapter 1: Birth & NICU Days:8

Ashwin's birth was far from the gentle, textbook delivery I had once envisioned. He arrived into the world small, frail, and fighting for life. The NICU became our temporary home, filled with beeping monitors, whispered prayers, and unrelenting hope.

He was administered Amikacin and Kanamycin to combat septicaemia — harsh names that etched themselves into my maternal memory. Too weak to suckle, he had to be fed breast milk through manual expression. I remember the pain — not just emotional but physical, as my hands swelled from engorgement and repeated efforts. It was my initiation into motherhood — raw, unfiltered, and fierce.

On the 19th day, Ashwin was discharged. We thought we had crossed the worst. My mother began caring for him while I resumed work, clutching a gnawing sense of unfinished worry.

When Ashwin was around three months old, he didn't turn his head to the harsh clatter of the washing machine. My husband — though not a doctor — noticed something wasn't right. Deep down, I knew too. We had him tested. The BERA (Brainstem Evoked Response Audiometry) confirmed our fears: profound sensorineural hearing loss. The blow came with another — that he might never speak, for speech needs hearing as its foundation.

While my husband was shattered and wanted to act immediately, I held on to one last thread of hope. We waited to meet the ENT specialist. He confirmed the diagnosis. He also advised me not to consider a second child, given the genetic uncertainties. That day, something within me quietly shifted. A storm of acceptance began to brew — one that would shape the mother I was about to become.

Ashwin's early months unfolded under the shadow of silence. Even as his tiny body grew, there was something profoundly quiet about his presence. We had already faced the diagnosis of profound hearing loss at three months. But the layers of complexity were just beginning to emerge.

Despite wearing hearing aids, his responses remained erratic. At ten months, I noticed he wasn't making eye contact. He didn't babble. There was no pointing, no reciprocal gestures, no mimicry. As a mother, I knew. As a doctor, I feared.

We visited developmental specialists. After thorough evaluations, the diagnosis came: Autism Spectrum Disorder. I wasn't shocked. It was as if my soul had been preparing me in fragments. But that didn't make it easier. The word 'autism' felt vast, unpredictable, and cruelly silent.

I remember walking out of the hospital that day and sitting quietly in the car. My husband didn't speak either. His dreams — our dreams — were quietly unraveling. But somewhere deep within, I also sensed this diagnosis wasn't an end. It was an entry point , into a new way of life, one that required fierce learning, unlearning, and unconditional presence.

Acceptance did not come overnight. I questioned everything , the antibiotics, the delivery, my karma. But slowly, I turned that questioning into seeking. Not just of treatments, but of meaning. I had a child who wouldn't speak in words, but who would one day teach me the language of patience, presence, and purpose.

Chapter 3: Building Inner Strength: pg 12

They say a mother becomes strong for her child. But in my case, it was Ashwin who became the reason I discovered a strength I never knew I had.

In the early days after his diagnosis, every task felt monumental. From navigating therapy centers to managing medical appointments, from learning sign language to decoding his cries — my life transformed into a disciplined surrender. There were no shortcuts, no weekends, no autopilot days. Every moment demanded attention.

But amid the chaos, a strange inner stillness began to emerge. It wasn't born from acceptance alone, but from the necessity to function. There was no time to wallow. Ashwin needed me to show up — not once, but repeatedly, patiently, silently.

I began to read, research, meditate. I practiced Pranic Healing and Reiki, not just for him, but for me. I needed emotional scaffolding, a way to patch up the invisible cracks forming under the pressure of motherhood, medicine, and meaning.

The outside world didn't always understand. I was often asked why I wasn't 'doing more' or 'trying alternative treatments.' But deep down, I knew the real healing lay not in fixing him — but in steadying myself.

And somewhere along the way, strength stopped feeling like a choice. It became second nature. Not loud. Not heroic. Just a quiet, firm, unwavering presence ,the kind that Ashwin could lean on. And I began to realize: resilience is not a medal we wear. It's the rhythm we adopt when love gives us no other option.

Autism doesn't just isolate the child — it isolates the family.

I realized this early when invitations to family functions slowed, conversations with friends became awkward, and even medical colleagues tiptoed around us with a politeness that stung more than silence. Society often doesn't reject you outright — it erases you subtly.

Ashwin's behavior was sometimes erratic in public. Meltdowns, flapping hands, vacant stares ,they attracted stares, whispers, and judgment. People offered advice we didn't ask for. Some blamed vaccines, some karma, others my parenting. I learned to carry both Ashwin and these societal projections.

But not all faces turned away. There were strangers who helped , like the kind Kashmiri horseman who guided him patiently on a solo ride, or the ashram caregivers who showed calm, structured love without ever asking 'why he's like this.' Their quiet compassion became my oxygen.

Family support, though often strained by emotional fatigue, was my grounding force. My sisters, my mother , they didn't always have answers, but they stood by. Anusha, Ashwin's cousin sister, treated him not as someone different, but as her brother unconditionally.

This chapter in our journey taught me that support is not about grand gestures. It's in the silent inclusion, the absence of judgment, the unspoken knowing. And stigma? It has power only when we believe in its sting. I began to armor myself not in defiance, but in quiet truth: we were not broken. Just different. And different deserves dignity too.

Ashwin's medical journey was not a single road but a maze. With every turn, we encountered new diagnoses, tests, therapies, and opinions — each offering a piece of a puzzle that never fully formed.

His profound hearing loss led to early discussions about cochlear implants. But we chose not to pursue surgery. It wasn't a straightforward case. Ashwin was already vulnerable, already neurologically atypical, and we didn't want to burden his fragile system further. No surgical intervention was done. And to this day, he has not vocalized a single word.

One day, Ashwin fell from the second floor of our apartment building. It was a nightmare no parent should ever witness. He was rushed to the emergency room, and investigations revealed a liver laceration. The prognosis was guarded, but surgery was not advised. He was kept in the ICU for a full week, monitored carefully to avoid even the slightest movement.

It was a week suspended in fear and silent prayers.

And then, something shifted. The bleeding stopped. The liver began healing. And within just one week, Ashwin — the same boy who had defied speech and structure — began to recover. Not through interventions, but through conservative care and quiet strength. It felt nothing short of a miracle.

His behavioral patterns, however, presented another layer of challenge. He would throw slippers repeatedly, break switches, bang his head against hard surfaces, and binge eat, sometimes even inducing vomiting afterward. These weren't tantrums — they were his way of releasing inner chaos. I came to understand them as desperate attempts at communication, control, or sensory relief.

There were no allergies. No pica. Just a child trying to make sense of his world , using his body as both instrument and expression.

And yet, even in that storm, there were breakthroughs , not the kind that made headlines, but ones that cracked open the heart. A tantrum avoided. A brief moment of stillness. A connection held just a little longer.

Medicine taught me how to read MRIs and lab results. But Ashwin taught me how to read the unspoken language of the body — the twitch of a lip, the flinch from a texture, the silent plea hidden in a gesture.

Those were the real breakthroughs. And they weren't prescribed ,they were patiently, prayerfully discovered.

Grace does not always descend in thunderclaps. Sometimes it comes through a kind teacher, a silent stranger, or a moment of unexpected peace.

There were days when Ashwin would smile for no reason, or walk calmly beside me after a stormy meltdown — moments I couldn't trace to any therapy or logic. They felt like divine whispers reminding me I wasn't alone.

Kodaikanal was one such turning point. We had gone there on a whim, and as Ashwin lay on the ground, staring into the sky, I saw bliss on his face. No sensory overload, no inner chaos ,just presence. I remember thinking, 'Why do we chase expensive cures when healing might just mean stillness?' That moment taught me that nature holds what no prescription can.

We also found warmth in Kashmir. The horseman who took Ashwin for a solo ride didn't flinch at his quirks. He simply accepted. That acceptance felt holier than a temple prayer.

The ashram stay though brief ,gave him structure, and gave me rest. Letting go wasn't easy, but returning was. I wanted him back. More importantly, he wanted to come back. It was a full circle drawn with invisible grace.

Even during the most turbulent phases, help came unannounced. In the form of a caring neighbor, a compassionate teacher, a silent hug. I began to see the divine not in rituals but in resilience — not in idols, but in everyday moments of grace.

Ashwin's journey may not have divine intervention in the dramatic sense. But every time I survived a night, found a resource, or felt a flicker of joy, I knew something higher was walking beside us , quietly, faithfully, gracefully.

Chapter 7: Autism and Hypersexuality : pg 20

Autism and hypersexuality — two words that rarely appear together in public discourse, yet in clinical reality, they sometimes intersect in challenging, confusing ways.

Autism Spectrum Disorder is often misunderstood as being associated with asexuality or low emotional response. But many autistic individuals do experience sexual urges ,sometimes heightened, sometimes atypically expressed. The challenge lies not in the presence of sexuality, but in the lack of social filters, delayed understanding of boundaries, and sensory-driven behaviors.

Ashwin began to exhibit hypersexual behaviors in adolescence. Touching, self-stimulation, inappropriate expressions , these weren't acts of defiance. They were signs of inner neurological confusion, of unmet sensory needs, and of limited understanding of social context.

Management required calm, consistent, and shame-free redirection. We avoided punishments. Instead, we focused on structured routines, private space for expression, and reducing triggers. Medical consultation ruled out hormonal imbalances and introduced behavior therapy strategies. It wasn't a quick fix , it was a practice in patience.

As a mother and a doctor, I had to drop the veil of embarrassment. His needs were natural, but the way he expressed them needed guidance. We spoke with therapists, caregivers, and families facing similar challenges. What emerged was a community of quiet warriors ,all navigating unspoken complexities with love and logic.

This chapter remains a work in progress. Hypersexuality in autism doesn't always go away, but with understanding and structure, it can be managed. More importantly, it deserves to be spoken about — not hidden. For every child like Ashwin, there must be safe spaces to grow , emotionally, physically, and yes, even sexually, with dignity.

Chapter 8: The Pillars Who Stood Tall:pg22

This book is for Ashwin—my karmic child, my teacher, and my purpose.

But behind my journey with him were my unwavering pillars of support,my husband and my brothers.

Their quiet strength deserves more than a passing mention. This chapter is my way of honouring them,those who stood tall behind the scenes, enabling me to carry Ashwin through every storm.

Looking back, I realise how much I leaned on these people who never sought the limelight, my husband and my brothers.

My husband, though occasionally reactive to stress (as most human beings are), never left me alone for even a single day to face Ashwin's temper tantrums. He has been my unwavering partner—starting from brushing Ashwin's teeth and bathing him, to feeding him and even helping with toilet needs. After my mother's death, it was he who shouldered the bulk of household duties, while still attending to Ashwin's special care. For this, I am indebted to him always.

I have seen many men walk away when faced with the reality of raising a differently-abled child. My husband stayed, not out of obligation, but out of quiet commitment. His selfless help should serve as an eye-opener for other men. When you marry a woman, you are not just entering into companionship,you are choosing to walk beside her through every phase of life. If you cannot offer that support, then it is better not to marry at all. Many women today would prefer to walk alone than carry the burden of a selfish partner in the name of marriage.

I am equally blessed when it comes to my brothers. All four of them were fond of Ashwin, but my youngest brother Natarajan (Nachu) has shown a depth of affection that deserves special mention. Their care has made my journey smoother in many ways. Nachu, in particular, continues to help me in every way he can, even now. I am truly grateful to have been born into a family where brothers continue to care deeply for their sisters.

It is easy to single out a mother's struggle in stories like mine. But the truth is,behind every strong mother who manages to smile through tears, there is often a silent army holding her up.

This chapter is for them

Chapter 9: Vedic Insight – Why Ashwin Was Born This Way : pg 24
The Vedas teach us that nothing in life is accidental — not even pain.

When I reflected on Ashwin's birth and journey through the lens of Vedic wisdom, I found a quiet acceptance growing within me. The doctrine of karma tells us that every soul chooses its circumstances — parents, challenges, even afflictions — as part of its evolution. Ashwin's soul, in this belief system, may have chosen this life not as a punishment, but as a path to purification and learning.

As his mother, I too may have been chosen , or I chose to walk this path. Perhaps it is the unfolding of my own karmic duties, my dharma. To serve without expectation. To mother without reward. To love without conditions. And in doing so, to cleanse layers of ego and attachment.

Some astrologers who read Ashwin's chart pointed to planetary placements that suggested a higher purpose. But I didn't need horoscopes to feel it. Every time I looked into his eyes, I saw a soul that was ancient , not broken. His silence wasn't emptiness; it was a stillness that echoed something beyond logic.

Vedic thought also speaks of 'atma-samarpanam' ,surrender of the self. Through Ashwin, I slowly began to surrender the version of life I thought I deserved, and embraced the life I was given. It wasn't lesser. It was just subtler , and perhaps, more sacred.

Not all mothers are chosen to walk this path. And not all souls take birth to teach. But I believe Ashwin's presence in my life is not a coincidence. It is cosmic choreography , one that unfolds beyond our comprehension, but never without meaning.

As a Radiologist, I've spent decades decoding the body's internal messages — images, shadows, contrasts. But when it came to autism, I realized that not all truths appear on scans.

One of the most common questions I face as both a doctor and a mother is: 'Could this have been detected earlier?' The honest answer is: not reliably. Autism is a neurodevelopmental condition, not a structural anomaly. Routine prenatal ultrasounds and postnatal imaging do not reveal it. There is no single blood test, scan, or MRI that can predict autism.

However, science is evolving. Advanced research in functional MRI and early brain patterning is beginning to identify subtle trends. But these are not yet clinically actionable, and certainly not definitive.

This gap in detection often causes guilt in parents. They revisit pregnancy scans, look for missed signs, or blame antibiotics or vaccines. I did too. But with time, I came to understand that autism is not always preventable. And it is certainly not anyone's fault.

As a Radiologist, I also want to reassure expectant mothers: your routine anomaly scans are not failing you. They are designed to detect life-threatening anomalies, not neurodiversity. The brain is a mystery even when magnified a thousand times.

Where radiology does help is in ruling out associated syndromes, guiding therapy, and occasionally catching rare metabolic or genetic markers. But the journey of autism diagnosis and support is still deeply clinical, behavioral, and personal.

This chapter is my attempt to bridge the medical and maternal,to clarify, comfort, and affirm that the absence of answers is not the absence of care. It is simply the present state of our scientific lens — ever evolving, just like our children.

If you're reading this and walking a similar path, let me tell you — you are not alone.

Autism isn't just a condition your child has. It's a journey your family takes. It redefines your pace, your priorities, your perspective. There will be days when progress seems invisible and nights when worry consumes sleep. But in between, there will be moments of grace — sometimes tiny, sometimes life-altering.

You will learn to celebrate what others take for granted — eye contact, a new word, a calm morning. You'll discover strength you didn't know lived inside you. You'll also cry — not always out of sorrow, but from the sheer beauty of a moment you never thought would arrive.

Please let go of comparisons. Your child is not behind. They are just on a different timeline — one that doesn't rush to meet anyone's expectations. Don't measure their worth, or yours, by society's milestones.

Accept help. Accept rest. Accept that some days will feel impossible. And know that love is not in how much you do, but in how fully you show up.

I want to take a moment here to thank those who walked with me , not just family, but those who became family through love. Ashwin feels Anil Kundra is his godfather, and Jyothi Ma'am his steady protector. When we had to step away briefly, they didn't just fill a role. They embraced a soul. To them, I owe more than gratitude. I owe peace.

This story has no perfect ending. Autism doesn't come with a cure. But it comes with clarity — of what truly matters, of what love really means.

Walk this path with courage. Walk it with compassion. And if some days all you can do is survive , that, too, is more than enough

Dr. Pankajam Rangarajan is not just a Radiologist , she is a mother, a seeker, a writer, and a woman who walked through fire with grace. Her journey with her son Ashwin, born with profound hearing loss and later diagnosed with autism, has redefined her understanding of medicine, motherhood, and the soul's deeper path.

With decades of experience in diagnostic imaging, Dr. Pankajam bridges the clinical with the emotional , blending science with silence, evidence with empathy. She is trained in Pranic Healing, Reiki, and Neuro-Linguistic Programming, allowing her to see healing not just through X-rays and MRIs, but through energy, language, and love.

Her writing style is reflective, honest, and rooted in lived experience. This book is not a prescription, but a presence — one that says: 'You are seen. You are supported. You are not alone.'

She continues to live and learn alongside Ashwin, drawing strength from his stillness, and sharing that strength with the world.

Tailpiece:31

"Let this be the closing frame — not of a story that ends,

but of one that continues quietly in the background.

Ashwin's journey is not for display, but for discovery —

one that unfolds in silence, love, and unseen strength.

This is not a conclusion, but a soft curtain drawn over a sacred space."

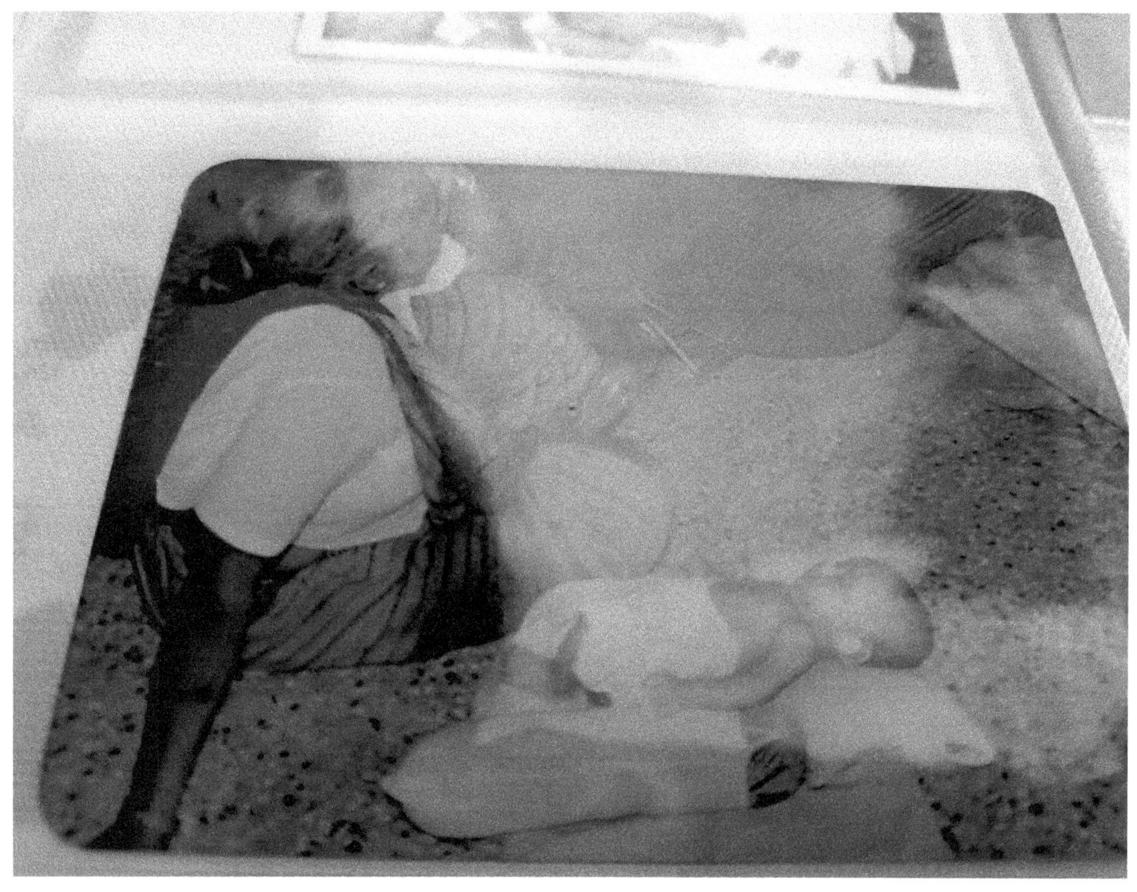

Sullen grandma in deep thought as to how my daughter will manage this kid with profound sensorineural hearing loss.

Ashwin's first birthday picture. Happy Ashwin.

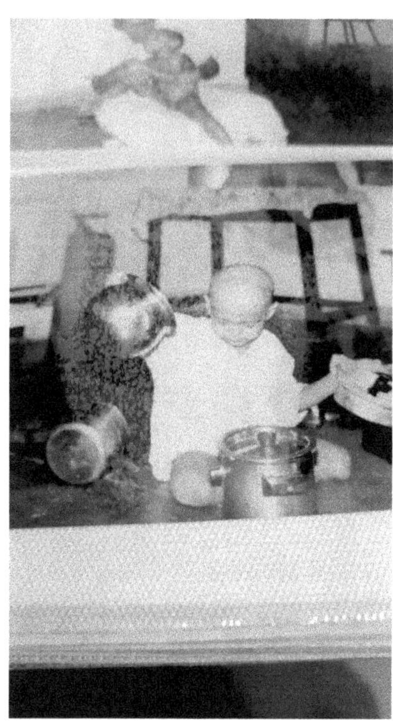

Early childhood – His unique style with vessels.

The famous balcony from where he fell

Ashwin being held by his father during naming ceremony
"From the very beginning, Appa stood by his side."

Ashwin embracing his father years later
"Through every storm, Appa remained his rock."

Ashwin with his surviving uncle
"Ashwin's dear uncle — still a source of warmth and strength."

Ashwin playing in the sea with his late uncle
"Pure joy — an uncle's love flowing like the waves."

Importance of family support.

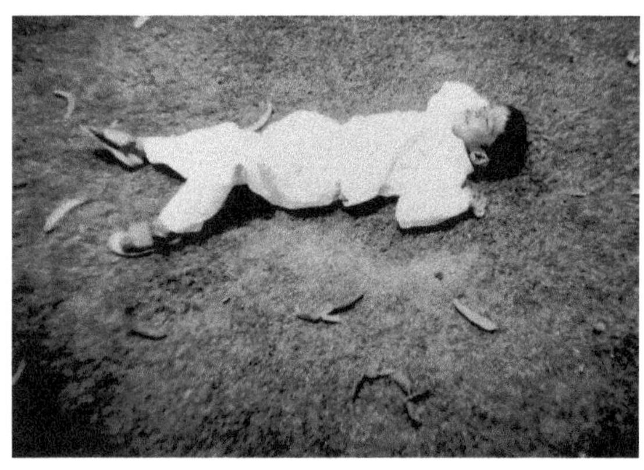

Ashwin's idea of bliss!

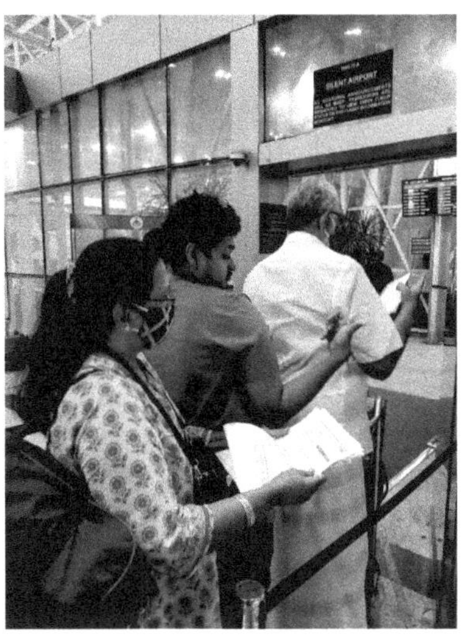

At Chennai airport 2020 for relocation to Hyderabad; settled happily at AGV, Hyderabad.

The worry of 'what after' is solved by entrusting Ashwin to Anil ji and Jyothi ma'am

www.ingramcontent.com/pod-product-compliance
Lightning Source LLC
Chambersburg PA
CBHW040220110726
48005CB00019B/3097